CW00391396

foreword

Chocolate chip, gingersnap, coconut, butterscotch—everyone has a favourite cookie. For some it's sugar cookies, so simple to decorate whatever the season, while others love the icebox kind, complete with memories of Grandmother's kitchen. These classic and updated treats from the library of Company's Coming are perfect for bake sales and instant pick-me-ups, and they're all here in this useful book.

It may sound counterintuitive, but for busy bakers, the freezer is an essential appliance. Mix up an extra batch of dough, double-wrap half and freeze for up to three months to bake later. Well-sealed baked cookies can be frozen for six to eight months. (The exception is macaroons, with a limit of two to three months.) Just make sure that any icing on cookies is completely dry, and that you layer them between waxed paper in an air-tight container. That way, you'll never run out of these delicious cookie-jar classics.

Jean Paré

pecan chip cookies

Pecans give these delicious chocolate chip cookies extra crunch, but even without nuts, these are fabulous. For chewy cookies, make sure you don't overbake.

Hard margarine (or butter), softened	1 cup	250 mL
Brown sugar, packed	1 1/2 cups	375 mL
Granulated sugar	1/2 cup	125 mL
Large eggs	2	2
Vanilla extract	1 1/2 tsp.	7 mL
All-purpose flour	2 1/2 cups	625 mL
Baking powder	1 tsp.	5 mL
Baking soda	1 tsp.	5 mL
Salt	1/2 tsp.	2 mL
Semi-sweet chocolate chips	2 cups	500 mL
Chopped pecans	1 cup	250 mL

Cream first 3 ingredients in large bowl. Add eggs 1 at a time, beating well after each addition. Add vanilla. Beat until smooth.

Combine next 4 ingredients in medium bowl. Add to margarine mixture in 2 additions, mixing well after each addition until no dry flour remains.

Add chocolate chips and pecans. Mix well. Drop, using 1 tbsp. (15 mL) for each, about 2 inches (5 cm) apart onto greased cookie sheets. Bake in 350°F (175°C) oven for about 10 minutes until edges are golden. Let stand on cookie sheets for 5 minutes. Remove cookies from cookie sheets and place on wire racks to cool. Makes about 84 cookies.

1 cookie: 87 Calories; 4.7 g Total Fat (2.6 g Mono, 0.6 g Poly, 1.4 g Sat); 5 mg Cholesterol; 11 g Carbohydrate; trace Fibre; 1 g Protein; 64 mg Sodium

orange and carrot cookies

Carrot cake isn't the only way to enjoy Bugs Bunny's favourite veggie. These chewy cookies are packed with good-for-you ingredients that will keep nibblers going till suppertime.

Large egg	1	1
Brown sugar, packed	1/3 cup	75 mL
Cooking oil	1/3 cup	75 mL
Grated carrot	1/2 cup	125 mL
Finely chopped pecans	1/3 cup	75 mL
Finely chopped pitted dates	1/3 cup	75 mL
Orange juice	1 tbsp.	15 mL
Grated orange zest	1 tsp.	5 mL
All-purpose flour	1 cup	250 mL
Baking powder	1 tsp.	5 mL
Salt	1/4 tsp.	1 mL

Beat egg and brown sugar in large bowl until thick and pale. Add cooking oil. Beat until smooth.

Add next 5 ingredients. Mix well.

Combine remaining 3 ingredients in small bowl. Add to carrot mixture. Stir until no dry flour remains. Drop, using 1 rounded tablespoonful for each, about 2 inches (5 cm) apart onto greased cookie sheets. Bake in 350°F (175°C) oven for about 15 minutes until golden. Let stand on cookie sheets for 5 minutes. Remove cookies from cookie sheets and place on wire racks to cool. Makes about 18 cookies.

1 cookie: 111 Calories; 6.2 g Total Fat (3.6 g Mono,1.7 g Poly, 0.5 g Sat); 12 mg Cholesterol; 13 g Carbohydrate; 1 g Fibre; 1 g Protein; 60 mg Sodium

chocolate chews

Warm, chocolatey cookies and a glass of cold chocolate milk—bring them on and watch the smiles appear!

Hard margarine (or butter), softened	1/2 cup	125 mL
Brown sugar, packed	1 cup	250 mL
Large egg	1	1
Unsweetened chocolate baking squares (1 oz., 28 g, each), chopped	2	2
Sour cream	1 cup	250 mL
Vanilla extract	1 tsp.	5 mL
All-purpose flour	1 3/4 cups	425 mL
Baking powder	2 tsp.	10 mL
Baking soda	1/2 tsp.	2 mL
Salt	1/4 tsp.	1 mL
Chopped walnuts	3/4 cup	175 mL

Cream margarine and brown sugar in large bowl. Add egg. Beat well.

Heat chocolate in small heavy saucepan on lowest heat, stirring often, until almost melted. Do not overheat. Remove from heat. Stir until smooth. Add to margarine mixture. Add sour cream and vanilla. Stir well.

Combine next 4 ingredients in small bowl. Add to chocolate mixture in 2 additions, mixing well after each addition until no dry flour remains.

Add walnuts. Mix well. Drop, using 1 tbsp. (15 mL) for each, about 1 inch (2.5 cm) apart onto greased cookie sheets. Bake in 375°F (190°C) oven for 10 to 12 minutes until edges are set. Let stand on cookie sheets for 5 minutes. Remove cookies from cookie sheets and place on wire racks to cool. Makes about 60 cookies.

1 cookie: 66 Calories; 1 g Protein; 3.9 g Total Fat (1.7 g Mono, 0.9 g Poly, 1.1 g Sat); 5 mg Cholesterol; 8 g Carbohydrate; trace Fibre; 1 g Protein; 47 mg Sodium

decadent chocolate chippers

Served fresh from the oven, the chunks of melting chocolate in these fabulous cookies are irresistible. Heaven!

Butter (or hard margarine), softened	1 cup	250 mL
Brown sugar, packed	1 1/2 cups	375 mL
Large eggs	2	2
Vanilla extract	1 tsp.	5 mL
All-purpose flour	2 cups	500 mL
Cornstarch	1/4 cup	60 mL
Baking soda	1 tsp.	5mL
Salt	3/4 tsp.	4 mL
Semi-sweet chocolate chunks	3 cups	750 mL
Coarsely chopped walnuts	2 cups	500 mL

Cream butter and brown sugar in large bowl. Add eggs, 1 at a time, beating well after each addition. Add vanilla. Beat until smooth.

Combine next 4 ingredients in small bowl. Add to butter mixture in 2 additions, mixing well after each addition until no dry flour remains.

Add chocolate chunks and walnuts. Mix well. Drop, using 1 1/2 tbsp. (25 mL) for each, about 2 inches (5 cm) apart onto greased cookie sheets. Bake in 350°F (175°C) oven for 10 to 15 minutes until golden. Let stand on cookie sheets for 5 minutes. Remove cookies from cookie sheets and place on wire racks to cool. Makes about 36 cookies.

1 cookie: 105 Calories; 4.8 g Total Fat (1.4 g Mono, 0.3 g Poly, 2.8 g Sat); 16 mg Cholesterol; 15 g Carbohydrate; 1 g Fibre; 2 g Protein; 78 mg Sodium

hazelnut cookies

Golden hazelnut cookies with spirals of icing on top. Delicious!

Butter (or hard margarine), softened	1/2 cup	125 mL
Brown sugar, packed	1 cup	250 mL
Large egg	1	1
Vanilla extract	1/2 tsp.	2 mL
All-purpose flour	2 cups	500 mL
Baking powder	3/4 tsp.	4 mL
Baking soda	3/4 tsp.	4 mL
Salt	1/4 tsp.	1 mL
Coarsely chopped hazelnuts (filberts), toasted (see Tip, page 64)	2/3 cup	150 mL
Sour cream	1/3 cup	75 mL
HAZELNUT ICING		
Butter (or hard margarine)	3 tbsp.	50 mL
Icing (confectioner's) sugar	1 cup	250 mL
Hazelnut liqueur	2 tbsp.	30 mL

Cream butter and brown sugar in large bowl. Add egg and vanilla. Beat well.

Combine next 4 ingredients in small bowl. Add to butter mixture in 2 additions, mixing well after each addition until no dry flour remains.

Add hazelnuts and sour cream. Mix well. Drop, using 2 tsp. (10 mL) for each, about 1 inch (2.5 cm) apart onto greased cookie sheets. Bake in 375°F (190°C) oven for 10 to 12 minutes until edges are golden. Let stand on cookie sheets for 5 minutes. Remove cookies from cookie sheets and place on wire racks to cool completely.

Hazelnut Icing: Melt butter in small saucepan on medium, stirring often, until golden. Remove from heat.

Beat in icing sugar and liqueur, adding more icing sugar or liqueur if necessary until spreading consistency. Makes about 1/2 cup (125 mL) icing. Spoon icing into piping bag fitted with small writing tip or small resealable bag with tiny piece snipped off corner. Pipe icing onto cookies. Makes about 72 cookies.

1 cookie: 62 Calories; 2.9 g Total Fat (1.2 g Mono, 0.2 g Poly, 1.4 g Sat); 9 mg Cholesterol; 8 g Carbohydrate; trace Fibre; 1 g Protein; 48 mg Sodium

chocolate coconut cookies

Cocoa in both the cookie and the icing will have chocolate lovers cheering.
This no-egg cookie dough will have a shortbread consistency.

Butter (or hard margarine), softened	3/4 cup	175 mL
Granulated sugar	1/3 cup	75 mL
All-purpose flour	1 1/2 cups	375 mL
Cocoa, sifted if lumpy	2 tbsp.	30 mL
Salt	1/4 tsp.	1 mL
Cornflakes cereal	1 cup	250 mL
Medium unsweetened coconut, toasted (see Tip, page 64)	1/3 cup	75 mL
CHOCOLATE ICING		
Icing (confectioner's) sugar	1 cup	250 mL
Milk	1 1/2 tbsp.	25 mL
Cocoa, sifted if lumpy	1 tbsp.	15 mL
Butter (or hard margarine), softened	2 tsp.	10 mL

Cream butter and sugar in large bowl until light and fluffy.

Combine next 3 ingredients in small bowl. Add to butter mixture in 2 additions, mixing well after each addition until no dry flour remains.

Add cereal and coconut. Mix well. Drop, using 1 tbsp. (15 mL) for each, about 1 inch (2.5 cm) apart onto greased cookie sheets. Bake in 350°F (175°C) oven for 10 to 12 minutes until edges are set. Let stand on cookie sheets for 5 minutes. Remove cookies from cookie sheets and place on wire racks to cool completely.

Chocolate Icing: Beat all 4 ingredients in small bowl, adding more icing sugar or milk if necessary until spreading consistency. Makes about 1/3 cup (75 mL) icing. Spoon icing into piping bag fitted with small writing tip or small resealable bag with tiny piece snipped off corner. Pipe icing onto cookies. Makes about 30 cookies.

1 cookie: 107 Calories; 6 g Total Fat (1.5 g Mono, 0.2 g Poly, 3.9 g Sat); 14 mg Cholesterol; 13 g Carbohydrate; trace Fibre; 1 g Protein; 82 mg Sodium

friendship cookies

A box of cake mix and a handful of ingredients is all you need. Fast enough to bake for old friends who drop by—easy enough to make often and give away, so you'll quickly gain new friends!

Large egg	1	1
Cooking oil	1/2 cup	125 mL
Box of chocolate cake mix (2 layer size)	1	1
Water	1/4 cup	60 mL
White chocolate chips	1 cup	250 mL

Beat egg and cooking oil in medium bowl until combined. Add cake mix and water. Beat until just moistened.

Add chocolate chips. Mix well. Drop, using 1 tbsp. (15 mL) for each, about 2 inches (5 cm) apart onto greased cookie sheets. Bake in 350°F (175°C) oven for 10 to 12 minutes until edges are set. Let stand on cookie sheets for 5 minutes. Remove cookies from cookie sheets and place on wire racks to cool. Makes about 48 cookies.

1 cookie: 85 Calories; 4.6 g Total Fat (2.3 g Mono, 0.9 g Poly, 1.2 g Sat); 5 mg Cholesterol; 11 g Carbohydrate; 0 g Fibre; 1 g Protein; 101 mg Sodium

hermits

An old favourite. The name comes from the fact that they taste even better if they're hidden for a day or two after baking. Good luck—their spicy aroma is sure to bring any hermit out of hiding! For an update, leave out the raisins and add the same amount of dried cranberries or chopped dried apricots.

Hard margarine (or butter), softened	1 cup	250 mL
Brown sugar, packed	1 1/2 cups	375 mL
Large eggs	3	3
Vanilla extract	1 tsp.	5 mL
All-purpose flour	3 cups	750 mL
Baking powder	1 tsp.	5 mL
Baking soda	1 tsp.	5 mL
Ground cinnamon	1 tsp.	5 mL
Ground nutmeg	1/2 tsp.	2 mL
Salt	1/2 tsp.	2 mL
Ground allspice	1/4 tsp.	1 mL
Chopped pitted dates	1 cup	250 mL
Raisins	1 cup	250 mL
Chopped walnuts (or your favourite nuts)	2/3 cup	150 mL

Cream margarine and brown sugar in large bowl. Add eggs 1 at a time, beating well after each addition. Add vanilla. Beat until smooth.

Combine next 7 ingredients in medium bowl. Add to margarine mixture in 3 additions, mixing well after each addition until no dry flour remains.

Add remaining 3 ingredients. Mix well. Drop, using 1 1/2 tbsp. (25 mL) for each, about 2 inches (5 cm) apart onto greased cookie sheets. Bake in 375°F (190°C) oven for 6 to 8 minutes until golden. Let stand on cookie sheets for 5 minutes. Remove cookies from cookie sheets and place on wire racks to cool. Makes about 48 cookies.

1 cookie: 130 Calories; 5.5 g Total Fat (3 g Mono, 1.2 g Poly, 1 g Sat); 13 mg Cholesterol; 19 g Carbohydrate; 1 g Fibre; 2 g Protein; 114 mg Sodium

coconut lime macaroons

These light, golden clusters are chewy on the inside and crunchy on the outside. If the macaroons stick to the cookie sheet, return them to the warm oven for a minute before trying to remove them.

Egg yolks (large)	2	2
Granulated sugar	2/3 cup	150 mL
Grated lime zest	1 tsp.	5 mL
Flaked coconut	1 3/4 cups	425 mL
Egg white (large)	1	1

Beat first 3 ingredients in large bowl for about 5 minutes until thick and pale.

Add coconut. Stir well.

Beat egg white in small bowl until stiff peaks form. Fold into coconut mixture until no white streaks remain. Drop, using 2 tsp. (10 mL) for each, about 2 inches (5 cm) apart onto parchment paper-lined cookie sheets. Bake on centre rack in 300°F (150°C) oven for 20 to 25 minutes until golden. Let stand on cookie sheets for 5 minutes. Remove cookies from cookie sheets and place on wire racks to cool. Makes about 30 cookies.

1 cookie: 44 Calories; 1.8 g Total Fat (0.2 g Mono, 0.1 g Poly, 1.4 g Sat); 14 mg Cholesterol; 7 g Carbohydrate; trace Fibre; trace Protein; 14 mg Sodium

butterscotch cookies

No need to turn on the oven for these crunchy treats.

Butterscotch chips	1 cup	250 mL
Smooth peanut butter	3 tbsp.	50 mL
Cornflakes cereal	3 cups	750 mL
Chopped pecans (or walnuts)	1/2 cup	125 mL

Heat butterscotch chips and peanut butter in large heavy saucepan on lowest heat, stirring often, until butterscotch chips are almost melted. Do not overheat. Remove from heat. Stir until smooth.

Add cereal and pecans. Mix well. Drop, using about 1 tbsp. (15 mL) for each, onto waxed paper-lined cookie sheets. Let stand until set. Makes about 30 cookies.

1 cookie: 53 Calories; 2.4 g Total Fat (1.3 g Mono, 0.6 g Poly, 0.3 g Sat); trace Cholesterol; 8 g Carbohydrate; trace Fibre; 1 g Protein; 36 mg Sodium

oatmeal chip cookies

The blend of chocolate, oatmeal and coconut make these a cookie-jar favourite.

Hard margarine (or butter), softened	1 cup	250 mL
Brown sugar, packed	2 cups	500 mL
Large eggs	2	2
Vanilla extract	1 tsp.	5 mL
All-purpose flour	2 cups	500 mL
Baking powder	1 tsp.	5 mL
Baking soda	1/2 tsp.	2 mL
Quick-cooking rolled oats	2 cups	500 mL
Semi-sweet chocolate chips	2 cups	500 mL
Medium unsweetened coconut	3/4 cup	175 mL

Cream margarine and brown sugar in large bowl. Add eggs 1 at a time, beating well after each addition. Add vanilla. Beat until smooth.

Combine next 3 ingredients in small bowl. Add to margarine mixture in 2 additions, mixing well after each addition until no dry flour remains.

Add remaining 3 ingredients. Mix well. Drop, using 2 tbsp. (30 mL) for each, about 2 inches (5 cm) apart onto greased cookie sheets. Bake in 350°F (175°C) oven for 8 to 10 minutes until golden. Let stand on cookie sheets for 5 minutes. Remove cookies from cookie sheets and place on wire racks to cool. Makes about 60 cookies.

1 cookie: 126 Calories; 6.2 g Total Fat (2.9 g Mono, 0.5 g Poly, 2.5 g Sat); 7 mg Cholesterol; 17 g Carbohydrate; 1 g Fibre; 2 g Protein; 61 mg Sodium

wartime cookies

Some cookies are born out of necessity and become classics. During the Second World War, when sugar was scarce, people substituted pudding powder and created these gems.

Hard margarine (or butter), softened	3/4 cup	175 mL
Box of butterscotch (or caramel) pudding powder (not instant), 6-serving size	1	1
Granulated sugar	1 tbsp.	15 mL
Large egg	1	1
Vanilla extract	1 tsp.	5 mL
Quick-cooking rolled oats	1 1/2 cups	375 mL
All-purpose flour	1 cup	250 mL
Baking powder	1/4 tsp.	1 mL
Baking soda	1/4 tsp.	1 mL
Salt	1/8 tsp.	0.5 mL

Cream first 3 ingredients in large bowl. Add egg and vanilla. Beat well.

Combine remaining 5 ingredients in medium bowl. Add to margarine mixture in 3 additions, mixing well after each addition until no dry flour remains. Roll into 1 inch (2.5 cm) balls. Arrange about 2 inches (5 cm) apart on greased cookie sheets. Flatten with fork. Bake in 375°F (190°C) oven for 10 to 15 minutes until golden. Let stand on cookie sheets for 5 minutes. Remove cookies from cookie sheets and place on wire racks to cool. Makes about 36 cookies.

1 cookie: 79 Calories; 4.5 g Total Fat (2.8 g Mono, 0.5 g Poly, 0.9 g Sat); 6 mg Cholesterol; 9 g Carbohydrate; trace Fibre; 1 g Protein; 79 mg Sodium

chocolate crunch cookies

Easy to make, with outstanding results. Crispy outside, chewy inside — so good!

Large eggs	2	2
Cooking oil	1/4 cup	60 mL
Box of devil's food cake mix	1	1
(2 layer size)		
Chocolate-covered buttery	3	3
toffee bars (1 1/2 oz., 39 g, each),		
coarsely chopped		

Beat eggs and cooking oil in medium bowl until combined. Add cake mix. Mix well.

Add chocolate bar pieces. Stir until combined. Roll into balls, using 2 tsp. (10 mL) for each. Arrange about 2 inches (5 cm) apart on greased cookie sheets. Bake in 350°F (175°C) oven for about 10 minutes until tops are cracked. Let stand on cookie sheets for 2 minutes. Remove cookies from cookie sheets and place on wire racks to cool. Makes about 48 cookies.

1 cookie: 69 Calories; 2.2 g Total Fat (0.9 g Mono, 0.4 g Poly, 0.7 g Sat); 10 mg Cholesterol; 2 g Carbohydrate; trace Fibre; 1 g Protein; 17 mg Sodium

cranberry chip cookies

The combination of tart cranberries, sweet white chocolate chips and unsalted peanuts makes this a fabulous-tasting cookie.

Large eggs	2	2
Brown sugar, packed	1 2/3 cups	400 mL
Cooking oil	1/2 cup	125 mL
Vanilla extract	1 tsp.	5 mL
All-purpose flour	1 3/4 cups	425 mL
Baking powder	1 tsp.	5 mL
Baking soda	1/2 tsp.	2 mL
Dried cranberries	1/2 cup	125 mL
Unsalted peanuts	1/2 cup	125 mL
White chocolate chips	1/2 cup	125 mL

Beat eggs and brown sugar in large bowl until thick and pale. Add cooking oil and vanilla. Beat until smooth.

Combine next 3 ingredients in small bowl. Add to egg mixture in 2 additions, mixing well after each addition until no dry flour remains.

Add remaining 3 ingredients. Mix well. Chill, covered, for 1 hour. Roll into balls, using 1 tbsp. (15 mL) for each. Arrange about 2 inches (5 cm) apart on greased cookie sheets. Bake in 350°F (175°C) oven for about 15 minutes until golden. Let stand on cookie sheets for 5 minutes. Remove cookies from cookie sheets and place on wire racks to cool. Makes about 42 cookies.

1 cookie: 107 Calories; 4.6 g Total Fat (2.4 g Mono, 1.2 g Poly, 0.8 g Sat); 11 mg Cholesterol; 16 g Carbohydrate; 1 g Fibre; 1 g Protein; 33 mg Sodium

nutri-cookies

Tell the kids they can have cookies for breakfast—they'll love it! Good as a between-activities snack when you're on the go. You can leave out the sunflower seeds and add 1/4 cup (60 mL) wheat germ as a variation.

Hard margarine (or butter), softened	1/2 cup	125 mL
Smooth peanut butter	1/2 cup	125 mL
Large eggs	2	2
Liquid honey	1 cup	250 mL
Vanilla extract	1 tsp.	5 mL
Quick-cooking rolled oats	3 cups	750 mL
All-purpose flour	1 1/2 cups	375 mL
Sultana raisins	1 cup	250 mL
Unsweetened medium coconut	1 cup	250 mL
Natural wheat bran	3/4 cup	175 mL
Chopped walnuts (or your favourite nuts)	1/2 cup	125 mL
Unsalted, roasted sunflower seeds	1/2 cup	125 mL
Baking soda	1 tsp.	5 mL
Salt	1 tsp.	5 mL

Cream margarine and peanut butter in large bowl. Add eggs 1 at a time, beating well after each addition. Add honey and vanilla. Beat until smooth.

Combine remaining 9 ingredients in medium bowl. Add to margarine mixture in 3 additions, mixing well after each addition until no dry flour remains. Roll into balls, using 1 tbsp. (15 mL) for each. Arrange about 2 inches (5 cm) apart on ungreased cookie sheets. Flatten slightly. Bake in 375°F (190°C) oven for about 12 minutes until golden. Let stand on cookie sheets for 5 minutes. Remove cookies from cookie sheets and place on wire racks to cool. Makes about 96 cookies.

1 cookie: *74 Calories; 3.5 g Total Fat (1.3 g Mono, 0.9 g Poly, 1.1 g Sat); 4 mg Cholesterol; 10 g Carbohydrate; 1 g Fibre; 2 g Protein; 59 mg Sodium*

mocha crinkles

These tantalizing cookies are the perfect blend of coffee and chocolate.
Try having just one!

Hard margarine (or butter), softened	1/2 cup	125 mL
Brown sugar, packed	1 cup	250 mL
Granulated sugar	3/4 cup	175 mL
Large eggs	3	3
Vanilla extract	1 1/2 tsp.	7 mL
Unsweetened chocolate baking squares (1 oz., 28 g, each), cut up	2	2
Instant coffee granules, crushed to fine powder	1 tbsp.	15 mL
All-purpose flour	2 cups	500 mL
Baking powder	1 1/2 tsp.	7 mL
Salt	1/2 tsp.	2 mL
Granulated sugar	1/3 cup	75 mL

Cream first 3 ingredients in large bowl. Add eggs 1 at a time, beating well after each addition. Add vanilla. Beat until smooth.

Heat chocolate and coffee granules in small heavy saucepan on lowest heat, stirring often, until chocolate is almost melted. Do not overheat. Remove from heat. Stir until smooth. Add to margarine mixture. Mix well.

Combine next 3 ingredients in medium bowl. Add to chocolate mixture in 2 additions, mixing well after each addition until no dry flour remains. Chill, covered, for at least 2 hours. Roll into 1 1/4 inch (3 cm) balls.

Roll balls in second amount of granulated sugar in shallow dish until coated. Arrange about 2 inches (5 cm) apart on greased cookie sheets. Bake in 350°F (175°C) oven for 10 to 12 minutes until tops are cracked. Cookies will be soft. Let stand on cookie sheets for 5 minutes. Remove cookies from cookie sheets and place on wire racks to cool. Makes about 42 cookies.

1 cookie: 98 Calories; 3.5 g Total Fat (1.9 g Mono, 0.3 g Poly, 1.0 g Sat); 15 mg Cholesterol; 16 g Carbohydrate; trace Fibre; 1 g Protein; 75 mg Sodium

famous cookies

Bring a plate of these oatmeal cookies studded with pecans and chocolate chips to your next potluck or fundraiser and watch them disappear—like celebrity guests, they show up and quickly vanish!

Hard margarine (or butter), softened	3/4 cup	175 mL
Brown sugar, packed	1/2 cup	125 mL
Granulated sugar	1/2 cup	125 mL
Large eggs	2	2
Vanilla extract	1/2 tsp.	2 mL
Quick-cooking rolled oats, processed in blender for 10 to 15 seconds	1 1/4 cups	300 mL
All-purpose flour	1 cup	250 mL
Baking powder	1/2 tsp.	2 mL
Baking soda	1/2 tsp.	2 mL
Salt	1/4 tsp.	1 mL
Semi-sweet chocolate chips	1 cup	250 mL
Chopped pecans	3/4 cup	175 mL
Sweet chocolate baking squares (1 oz., 28 g, each), grated	2	2

Cream first 3 ingredients in large bowl. Add eggs 1 at a time, beating well after each addition. Add vanilla. Beat until smooth.

Combine next 5 ingredients in medium bowl. Add to margarine mixture in 2 additions, mixing well after each addition until no dry flour remains.

Add remaining 3 ingredients. Mix well. Roll into 1 1/4 inch (3 cm) balls. Arrange about 2 inches (5 cm) apart on greased cookie sheets. Bake in 375°F (190°C) oven for about 10 minutes until edges are golden. Let stand on cookie sheets for 5 minutes. Remove cookies from cookie sheets and place on wire racks to cool. Makes about 60 cookies.

1 cookie: 84 Calories; 5 g Total Fat (2.7 g Mono, 0.6 g Poly, 1.4 g Sat); 7 mg Cholesterol; 10 g Carbohydrate; 1 g Fibre; 1 g Protein; 56 mg Sodium

giant toffee bar cookies

These often don't make it from the cookie sheet to the cookie jar! You can make smaller cookies by rolling out smaller balls, but they'll take less time to bake.

Hard margarine (or butter), softened	1 cup	250 mL
Brown sugar, packed	1 cup	250 mL
Granulated sugar	1 cup	250 mL
Large eggs	2	2
Vanilla extract	2 tsp.	10 mL
All-purpose flour	2 cups	500 mL
Baking powder	1 tsp.	5 mL
Baking soda	1 tsp.	5 mL
Salt	1/2 tsp.	2 mL
Quick-cooking rolled oats	2 1/3 cups	575 mL
Chocolate-covered buttery toffee bars (1 1/2 oz., 39 g, each), coarsely chopped	8	8
Granulated sugar	1/4 cup	60 mL

Cream first 3 ingredients in large bowl. Add eggs 1 at a time, beating well after each addition. Add vanilla. Beat until smooth.

Combine next 4 ingredients in small bowl. Add to margarine mixture in 2 additions, mixing well after each addition until no dry flour remains.

Add rolled oats and chocolate bar pieces. Mix well. Roll into 2 inch (5 cm) balls. Arrange about 4 inches (10 cm) apart on greased cookie sheets.

Dip flat-bottomed glass into second amount of granulated sugar. Flatten balls to 1/2 inch (12 mm) thickness, dipping glass in granulated sugar as necessary. Bake in 375°F (190°C) oven for 10 to 12 minutes until golden. Let stand on cookie sheets for 5 minutes. Remove cookies from cookie sheets and place on wire racks to cool. Makes about 36 cookies.

1 cookie: 204 Calories; 9.2 g Total Fat (3.8 g Mono, 0.8 g Poly, 1.3 g Sat); 17 mg Cholesterol; 29 g Carbohydrate; 1 g Fibre; 3 g Protein; 168 mg Sodium

peanut blossoms

Chocolate centres make these awesome blossoms look a bit like flowers.
And who can resist the combination of chocolate and peanut butter?

Hard margarine (or butter), softened	1/2 cup	125 mL
Smooth peanut butter	1/2 cup	125 mL
Brown sugar, packed	1/2 cup	125 mL
Granulated sugar	1/2 cup	125 mL
Large egg	1	1
Milk	2 tbsp.	30 mL
Vanilla extract	1 tsp.	5 mL
All-purpose flour	1 3/4 cups	425 mL
Baking soda	1 tsp.	5 mL
Salt	1/2 tsp.	2 mL
Granulated sugar, approximately	1/3 cup	75 mL
Milk chocolate kisses, approximately	54	54

Cream first 4 ingredients in large bowl. Add next 3 ingredients. Mix well.

Combine next 3 ingredients in small bowl. Add to peanut butter mixture in 2 additions, mixing well after each addition until no dry flour remains. Roll into 1 inch (2.5 cm) balls.

Roll balls in second amount of granulated sugar in same small bowl until coated. Arrange about 2 inches (5 cm) apart on ungreased cookie sheets. Bake in 375°F (190°C) oven for about 10 minutes until golden. Remove from oven.

Immediately place 1 chocolate kiss on top of each cookie. Press down until cookie cracks around edge. Let stand on cookie sheets for 5 minutes. Remove cookies from cookie sheets and place on wire racks to cool. Makes about 54 cookies.

1 cookie: 90 Calories; 4.4 g Total Fat (2.2 g Mono, 0.6 g Poly, 1.4 g Sat); 5 mg Cholesterol; 12 g Carbohydrate; trace Fibre; 2 g Protein; 84 mg Sodium

gingersnaps

Good gingersnaps have a bit of a bite to them. Make sure your ground ginger and cinnamon are fresh; otherwise you'll end up with cookies with no "snap."

Hard margarine (or butter), softened	3/4 cup	175 mL
Granulated sugar	1 cup	250 mL
Large egg	1	1
Fancy (mild) molasses	1/2 cup	125 mL
All-purpose flour	2 1/2 cups	625 mL
Baking soda	2 tsp.	10 mL
Ground ginger	2 tsp.	10 mL
Ground cinnamon	1 tsp.	5 mL
Salt	1/2 tsp.	2 mL
Granulated sugar, approximately	1/4 cup	60 mL

Cream margarine and first amount of sugar in large bowl. Add egg and molasses. Beat well.

Combine next 5 ingredients in medium bowl. Add to margarine mixture in 2 additions, mixing well after each addition until no dry flour remains. Roll into 1 inch (2.5 cm) balls.

Roll balls in second amount of sugar in small bowl until coated. Arrange about 2 inches (5 cm) apart on greased cookie sheets. Bake in 350°F (175°C) oven for about 10 minutes until just set. Let stand on cookie sheets for 5 minutes. Remove cookies from cookie sheets and place on wire racks to cool. Makes about 90 cookies.

1 cookie: 45 Calories; 1.7 g Total Fat (1.1 g Mono, 0.2 g Poly, 0.4 g Sat); 2 mg Cholesterol; 7 g Carbohydrate; trace Fibre; trace Protein; 62 mg Sodium

big batch rainbow chip cookies

Got a bake sale coming up? This recipe makes about 13 dozen flourless cookies! Use an extra-large bowl or roasting pan to mix these. Pressed for time? Divide the dough into smaller portions, bake what you need and freeze the rest in a double layer of plastic wrap. But if you're in a real baking mood, this recipe can be doubled.

Hard margarine (or butter), softened	1 cup	250 mL
Smooth peanut butter	3 cups	750 mL
Brown sugar, packed	3 cups	750 mL
Granulated sugar	2 cups	500 mL
Large eggs	6	6
Golden corn syrup	1/2 tbsp.	7 mL
Vanilla extract	1/2 tbsp.	7 mL
Quick-cooking rolled oats	9 cups	2.25 L
Candy-coated chocolate candies	1 cup	250 mL
Semi-sweet chocolate chips	1 cup	250 mL
Baking soda	4 tsp.	20 mL

Beat first 4 ingredients in extra-large bowl until light and creamy. Add eggs 2 at a time, beating well after each addition. Add corn syrup and vanilla. Beat until smooth.

Add remaining 4 ingredients. Mix well. Roll into balls, using 2 tbsp. (30 mL) for each. Arrange about 2 inches (5 cm) apart on greased cookie sheets. Flatten slightly. Bake in 350°F (175°C) oven for 7 to 8 minutes until golden. Let stand on cookie sheets for 5 minutes. Remove cookies from cookie sheets and place on wire racks to cool. Makes about 156 cookies.

1 cookie: 108 Calories; 5.2 g Total Fat (2.4 g Mono, 1 g Poly, 1.1 g Sat); 8 mg Cholesterol; 14 g Carbohydrate; 1 g Fibre; 3 g Protein; 78 mg Sodium

paintbox cookies

Every cookie looks different in this recipe—choose different colours to suit the occasion. You can play with the number of ropes you use at one time. For striped cookies, just lay contrasting ropes next to each other, but DON'T twist them before you roll them out.

Hard margarine (or butter), softened	1 cup	250 mL
Granulated sugar	1 1/2 cups	375 mL
Large eggs	2	2
Liquid honey	1/4 cup	60 mL
Vanilla extract	2 tsp.	10 mL
Hot water	1 1/2 tbsp.	25 mL
Baking soda	1 tbsp.	15 mL
All-purpose flour	4 1/2 cups	1.1 L

Paste food colouring (see Tip, page 64),
  assorted colours

Cream margarine and sugar in large bowl. Add eggs 1 at a time, beating well after each addition. Add honey and vanilla. Beat until smooth.

Stir hot water into baking soda in small dish. Add to margarine mixture. Mix well.

Add flour in 4 additions, mixing well after each addition until no dry flour remains. Divide dough into 4 or 5 equal portions. Knead enough food colouring into each portion of dough until desired shade (see Tip, page 64). Divide each portion in half. Roll out each portion into 16 inch (40 cm) long rope. Lay a few different coloured ropes on top of each other. Twist gently into 1 rope. Roll out on lightly floured surface to 1/4 inch (6 mm) thickness. Cut out shapes with lightly floured 2 inch (5 cm) cookie cutter. Roll out scraps to cut more shapes. Arrange shapes about 2 inches (5 cm) apart on greased cookie sheets. Bake in 350°F (175°C) oven for 8 to 10 minutes until set. Let stand on cookie sheets for 5 minutes. Remove cookies from cookie sheets and place on wire racks to cool. Repeat with remaining dough. Makes about 72 cookies.

1 cookie: *77 Calories; 2.9 g Total Fat (1.8 g Mono, 0.3 g Poly, 0.6 g Sat); 6 mg Cholesterol; 12 g Carbohydrate; trace Fibre; 1 g Protein; 83 mg Sodium*

sugar cookies

A very good, versatile cookie to use with whatever cookie cutters you have on hand. For a "sweet" birthday party activity, have the kids decorate them to take home as party favours. Use your favourite coloured icing, gels, dragées and decorating sugar.

Hard margarine (or butter), softened	3/4 cup	175 mL
Granulated sugar	3/4 cup	175 mL
Large egg	1	1
Vanilla extract	1 tsp.	5 mL
All-purpose flour	2 cups	500 mL
Baking soda	1 tsp.	5 mL
Cream of tartar	1 tsp.	5 mL
Salt	1/4 tsp.	1 mL
Ground cardamom (optional)	1/4 tsp.	1 mL

Cream margarine and sugar in large bowl. Add egg and vanilla. Beat well.

Combine remaining 5 ingredients in small bowl. Add to margarine mixture in 2 additions, mixing well after each addition until no dry flour remains. Divide into 2 equal portions. Shape each portion into flattened disc. Wrap each with waxed paper. Chill for at least 6 hours or overnight. Discard waxed paper from 1 disc. Roll out dough on lightly floured surface to 1/8 inch (3 mm) thickness. Cut out shapes with lightly floured 2 inch (5 cm) cookie cutter. Roll out scraps to cut more shapes. Arrange shapes about 2 inches (5 cm) apart on greased cookie sheets. Bake in 350°F (175°C) oven for about 10 minutes until edges are just golden. Let stand on cookie sheets for 5 minutes. Remove cookies from cookie sheets and place on wire racks to cool. Repeat with remaining disc. Makes about 84 cookies.

1 cookie: 35 Calories; 1.8 g Total Fat (1.2 g Mono, 0.2 g Poly, 0.4 g Sat); 3 mg Cholesterol; 4 g Carbohydrate; trace Fibre; trace Protein; 43 mg Sodium

raisin-filled cookies

Get your fill of raisins with these scrumptious treats. Excellent with ice cream for dessert!

Coarsely chopped raisins	1 1/4 cups	300 mL
Granulated sugar	1/2 cup	125 mL
Water	1/2 cup	125 mL
Cornstarch	2 tsp.	10 mL
Lemon juice	1 tsp.	5 mL
Hard margarine (or butter), softened	1 cup	250 mL
Granulated sugar	1 1/2 cups	375 mL
Large eggs	2	2
Vanilla extract	1 tsp.	5 mL
All-purpose flour	3 1/2 cups	875 mL
Baking soda	1 tsp.	5 mL
Salt	1/2 tsp.	2 mL

Granulated sugar, for decorating

Combine first 5 ingredients in medium saucepan. Bring to a boil on medium. Boil gently for 5 minutes, stirring occasionally. Remove from heat. Cool.

Cream margarine and second amount of sugar in large bowl. Add eggs 1 at a time, beating well after each addition. Add vanilla. Beat until smooth.

Combine next 3 ingredients in medium bowl. Add to margarine mixture in 3 additions, mixing well after each addition until no dry flour remains. Divide into 2 equal portions. Roll out 1 portion on lightly floured surface to 1/4 inch (6 mm) thickness. Cut out circles with lightly floured 2 1/2 inch (6.4 cm) round cookie cutter. Roll out scraps to cut more circles. Spread about 1 tsp. (5 mL) raisin mixture evenly on half of circles, leaving 1/4 inch (6 mm) edge. Place remaining circles on top of raisin mixture. Press edges together with fork to seal. Arrange about 2 inches (5 cm) apart on greased cookie sheets. Carefully cut 1/2 inch (12 mm) "X" in top of each cookie.

Sprinkle cookies with sugar. Bake in 350°F (175°C) oven for about 10 minutes until golden. Let stand on cookie sheets for 5 minutes. Remove cookies from cookie sheets and place on wire racks to cool. Repeat with remaining dough portion, raisin mixture and sugar. Makes about 36 cookies.

1 cookie: 161 Calories; 5.8 g Total Fat (3.6 g Mono, 0.6 g Poly, 1.2 g Sat); 12 mg Cholesterol; 26 g Carbohydrate; 1 g Fibre; 2 g Protein; 136 mg Sodium

lemon icebox cookies

Deliciously crisp, with a lovely citrus glaze drizzled on top. As a variation, slightly flatten the logs to create square logs, chill, cut and bake as directed. Leave out the lemon glaze. Instead, dip half of each cookie into melted chocolate and let set on waxed paper.

Hard margarine (or butter), softened	1 cup	250 mL
Granulated sugar	3/4 cup	175 mL
Large eggs	2	2
Grated lemon zest	1 tbsp.	15 mL
All-purpose flour	3 cups	750 mL
Baking powder	1/2 tsp.	2 mL
Salt	1/4 tsp.	1 mL
LEMON GLAZE		
Lemon juice	1 – 2 tbsp.	15 – 30 mL
Icing (confectioner's) sugar	1/2 cup	125 mL
Drop of yellow liquid food colouring (optional)	1	1

Cream margarine and sugar in large bowl. Add eggs 1 at a time, beating well after each addition. Add lemon zest. Beat until smooth.

Combine next 3 ingredients in medium bowl. Add to margarine mixture in 3 additions, mixing well after each addition until no dry flour remains. Divide into 2 equal portions. Shape each portion into 8 inch (20 cm) long log. Wrap each log with waxed paper. Chill for at least 6 hours or overnight. Discard waxed paper from 1 log. Cut into 1/4 inch (6 mm) slices. Arrange slices about 2 inches (5 cm) apart on ungreased cookie sheets. Bake in 375°F (190°C) oven for 7 to 10 minutes until edges are golden. Let stand on cookie sheets for 5 minutes. Remove cookies from cookie sheets and place on wire racks to cool completely. Repeat with remaining log.

Lemon Glaze: Stir lemon juice into icing sugar in small bowl, adding more lemon juice or icing sugar if necessary until pourable consistency. Add food colouring. Mix well. Makes about 1/4 cup (60 mL) glaze. Spoon glaze into piping bag fitted with small writing tip or small resealable bag with tiny piece snipped off corner. Pipe glaze onto cookies. Let stand until set. Makes about 60 cookies.

1 cookie: 70 Calories; 3.5 g Total Fat (2.2 g Mono, 0.4 g Poly, 0.7 g Sat); 7 mg Cholesterol; 9 g Carbohydrate; trace Fibre; 1 g Protein; 53 mg Sodium

sesame ginger cookies

Tasty, buttery cookies with ginger and sesame seeds. You can double-wrap the logs and freeze them for fresh-baked cookies any time—make sure to thaw the dough for 30 minutes before slicing.

Butter (or hard margarine), softened	1/2 cup	125 mL
Brown sugar, packed	1 cup	250 mL
Large egg	1	1
Vanilla extract	1 tsp.	5 mL
All-purpose flour	1 1/2 cups	375 mL
Sesame seeds, toasted (see Tip, page 64)	1/4 cup	60 mL
Baking powder	1 tsp.	5 mL
Ground ginger	1/2 tsp.	2 mL
Salt	1/4 tsp.	1 mL
Sesame seeds, toasted (see Tip, page 64)	1/3 cup	75 mL

Cream butter and brown sugar in large bowl. Add egg and vanilla. Beat well.

Combine next 5 ingredients in small bowl. Add to butter mixture. Mix well. Divide into 2 equal portions. Shape each portion into 8 inch (20 cm) long log. Slightly flatten both round logs to create squared logs.

Press logs firmly into second amount of sesame seeds to coat all sides. Wrap each log with waxed paper. Chill for at least 3 hours. Discard waxed paper from 1 log. Cut into 1/4 inch (6 mm) slices. Arrange slices about 2 inches (5 cm) apart on greased cookie sheets. Bake in 350°F (175°C) oven for about 12 minutes until edges are golden. Let stand on cookie sheets for 5 minutes. Remove cookies from cookie sheets and place on wire racks to cool. Repeat with remaining log. Makes about 64 cookies.

1 cookie: 48 Calories; 2.3 g Total Fat (0.7 g Mono, 0.4 g Poly, 1.1 g Sat); 7 mg Cholesterol; 6 g Carbohydrate; trace Fibre; 1 g Protein; 34 mg Sodium

oatmeal dippers

Cookie monsters will love dipping these delights into applesauce or pudding!

Hard margarine (or butter), softened	1/2 cup	125 mL
Brown sugar, packed	1/2 cup	125 mL
Large egg	1	1
Vanilla extract	1 tsp.	5 mL
Quick-cooking rolled oats	1 cup	250 mL
Medium sweetened coconut	1/2 cup	125 mL
Whole wheat flour	1/2 cup	125 mL
Natural oat bran	1/4 cup	60 mL
Baking soda	1/2 tsp.	2 mL
Ground cinnamon	1/2 tsp.	2 mL
Salt	1/4 tsp.	1 mL

Cream margarine and brown sugar in large bowl. Add egg and vanilla. Beat well.

Combine remaining 7 ingredients in medium bowl. Add to margarine mixture in 2 additions, mixing well after each addition until no dry flour remains. Press evenly into waxed paper-lined 8 x 8 inch (20 x 20 cm) pan. Chill for 1 hour. Invert onto cutting board. Discard waxed paper. Cut oat mixture in half. Cut each half crosswise into 12 pieces, for a total of 24 pieces. Arrange pieces about 1 inch (2.5 cm) apart on greased cookie sheets. Bake in 350°F (175°C) oven for about 10 minutes until golden. Let stand on cookie sheets for 5 minutes. Remove cookies from cookie sheets and place on wire racks to cool. Makes 24 cookies.

1 cookie: 94 Calories; 5.2 g Total Fat (2.9 g Mono, 0.6 g Poly, 1.4 g Sat); 9 mg Cholesterol; 11 g Carbohydrate; 1 g Fibre; 2 g Protein; 108 mg Sodium

banana bread dunkers

Pack a few of these low-fat banana biscotti along for the morning coffee break. Be careful: you may have to share!

All-purpose flour	2 cups	500 mL
Whole wheat flour	1/2 cup	125 mL
Baking soda	1 tsp.	5 mL
Salt	1/4 tsp.	1 mL
Hard margarine (or butter), softened	1/4 cup	60 mL
Brown sugar, packed	1/3 cup	75 mL
Large eggs	2	2
Egg white (large)	1	1
Mashed banana (about 1 large)	1/2 cup	125 mL
Vanilla extract	1 tsp.	5 mL

Measure first 4 ingredients into large bowl. Stir. Make a well in centre. Set aside.

Cream margarine and brown sugar in medium bowl. Add eggs 1 at a time, beating well after each addition. Add egg white. Beat well.

Add banana and vanilla. Beat well. Add to well in flour mixture. Mix until soft dough forms. Turn out onto lightly floured surface. Knead 6 times. Shape into 16 inch (40 cm) long log. Place on greased cookie sheet. Flatten slightly. Bake in 350°F (175°C) oven for about 30 minutes until golden. Let stand on cookie sheet for about 15 minutes until cool enough to handle. Cut log diagonally with serrated knife into 1/2 inch (12 mm) slices. Cut each slice in half. Arrange slices about 2 inches (5 cm) apart on 2 ungreased cookie sheets. Bake on separate racks in 275°F (140°C) oven for 10 minutes, switching position of pans at halftime. Turn slices over. Turn oven off. Let stand in oven for about 30 minutes until dry and crisp. Remove cookies from cookie sheets and place on wire racks to cool. Makes about 48 cookies.

1 cookie: *46 Calories; 1.3 g Total Fat (0.8 g Mono, 0.2 g Poly, 0.3 g Sat); 9 mg Cholesterol; 7 g Carbohydrate; trace Fibre; 1 g Protein; 56 mg Sodium*

almond jelly swirls

Fruit jelly spirals through these sugar cookies, to eye-catching effect.

Butter (or hard margarine), softened	1/2 cup	125 mL
Granulated sugar	1 cup	250 mL
Large egg	1	1
Milk	3 tbsp.	50 mL
Almond extract	1/2 tsp.	2 mL
All-purpose flour	2 2/3 cups	650 mL
Baking powder	1/2 tsp.	2 mL
Salt	1/4 tsp.	1 mL
Blackcurrant jelly (or blackberry jam)	1/2 cup	125 mL
Cornstarch	1 tsp.	5 mL
Finely chopped sliced almonds, toasted (see Tip, page 64)	1/3 cup	75 mL

Cream butter and sugar in large bowl. Add next 3 ingredients. Beat well.

Combine next 3 ingredients in medium bowl. Add to butter mixture in 2 additions, mixing well after each addition until no dry flour remains. Divide into 2 equal portions. Cover each portion with plastic wrap. Chill for at least 3 hours.

Stir jelly into cornstarch in small saucepan. Heat and stir on medium for about 3 minutes until bubbling. Remove from heat. Let stand, covered, until cooled completely. Roll out 1 portion of dough between 2 sheets of waxed paper to 8 x 12 inch (20 x 30 cm) rectangle. Place dough on baking sheet. Chill for 30 minutes. Remove top piece of waxed paper. Spread half of jelly mixture evenly over dough to edge.

Sprinkle with half of almonds. Roll up tightly, jelly roll-style, from short side, using waxed paper as guide. Press seam against roll to seal. Wrap tightly with plastic wrap. Repeat with remaining portion of dough, jelly mixture and almonds. Chill for at least 6 hours. Cut rolls into 1/4 inch (6 mm) slices. Arrange slices about 2 inches (5 cm) apart on greased cookie sheets. Bake in 375°F (190°C) oven for 12 to 14 minutes until edges are golden. Let stand on cookie sheets for 5 minutes. Remove cookies from cookie sheets and place on wire racks to cool. Makes about 60 cookies.

1 cookie: 54 Calories; 2 g Total Fat (0.6 g Mono, 0.2 g Poly, 1 g Sat); 7 mg Cholesterol; 8 g Carbohydrate; trace Fibre; 1 g Protein; 28 mg Sodium

crowd-pleasing cookie pizza

OK, this won't fit into a cookie jar, but it's such a fun party dessert! You could also put it in a pretty box as a welcome gift.

CRUST

Hard margarine (or butter), softened	1/2 cup	125 mL
Brown sugar, packed	3/4 cup	175 mL
Large egg	1	1
Vanilla extract	1 tsp.	5 mL
All-purpose flour	1 1/2 cups	375 mL

TOPPING

Milk chocolate chips	1 cup	250 mL
Miniature marshmallows	1 cup	250 mL
Finely chopped pecans (optional)	1/2 cup	125 mL
Can of sweetened condensed milk	11 oz.	300 mL
Candy-coated chocolate candies	1/2 cup	125 mL

Crust: Cream margarine and brown sugar in large bowl. Add egg and vanilla. Beat well.

Add flour. Mix until no dry flour remains. Turn out onto lightly floured surface. Knead for 5 minutes. Press dough into greased 12 inch (30 cm) pizza pan, forming rim around edge.

Topping: Sprinkle first 3 ingredients, in order given, evenly over crust. Pour condensed milk evenly over top. Bake in 350°F (175°C) oven for about 20 minutes until crust is golden.

Immediately arrange candies on top. Cool completely in pan. Cuts into 16 wedges.

1 wedge: 321 Calories; 13.4 g Total Fat (5.8 g Mono, 0.9 g Poly, 4.7 g Sat); 25 mg Cholesterol; 47 g Carbohydrate; 1 g Fibre; 5 g Protein; 127 mg Sodium

recipe index

topical tips

Cooling cookie sheets: It's a good idea to cool cookie sheets between batches; otherwise recipe times or cookie shapes may be changed by a too-hot cookie sheet.

Eliminating food colouring stains: To avoid staining your hands with the food colouring, wear disposable plastic gloves when kneading.

Finding good food colouring: Paste food colouring gives a wider variety of vivid colours. It can be purchased at craft or cake decorating stores.

Toasting nuts, seeds or coconut: Cooking times will vary for each type of nut—so never toast them together. For small amounts, place ingredient in an ungreased shallow frying pan. Heat on medium for three to five minutes, stirring often, until golden. For larger amounts, spread ingredient evenly in an ungreased shallow pan. Bake in 350°F (175°C) oven for five to 10 minutes, stirring or shaking often, until golden.

Nutrition Information Guidelines

Each recipe is analyzed using the Canadian Nutrient File from Health Canada, which is based on the United States Department of Agriculture (USDA) Nutrient Database.

- If more than one ingredient is listed (such as "butter or hard margarine"), or if a range is given (1 – 2 tsp., 5 – 10 mL), only the first ingredient or first amount is analyzed.

- For meat, poultry and fish, the serving size per person is based on the recommended 4 oz. (113 g) uncooked weight (without bone), which is 2 – 3 oz. (57 – 85 g) cooked weight (without bone)— approximately the size of a deck of playing cards.

- Milk used is 1% M.F. (milk fat), unless otherwise stated.

- Cooking oil used is canola oil, unless otherwise stated.

- Ingredients indicating "sprinkle," "optional" or "for garnish" are not included in the nutrition information.

- The fat in recipes and combination foods can vary greatly depending on the sources and types of fats used in each specific ingredient. For these reasons, the count of saturated, monounsaturated and polyunsaturated fats may not add up to the total fat content.